Farm and Ranch Animals Coloring Book

Educational and Relaxing Fun for Kids and Adults

By Candie Witherspoon

All designs, text and illustrations Copyright © 2022 by Candie Witherspoon.
ALL RIGHTS RESERVED. ISBN: 9798374328127

No part of this book may be copied, reproduced or distributed without the written consent of the author and illustrator.

This book belongs to:

Welcome to Farmer Mike's farm and ranch!

You will get to see all the different animals that live here.

You may have some of these animals living at your home or farm too.

Every farm and ranch is a little different. Some have many different kinds of animals and some specialize in one or two.

Farmer Mike has the biggest variety of animals and it sometimes looks more like a zoo than a ranch or farm.

Let's begin our adventure by meeting Farmer Mike and his family.

Farmer Mike has 22 different kinds of animals that he raises and takes care of on his farm and ranch.

How many can you identify? Can you name all of them?

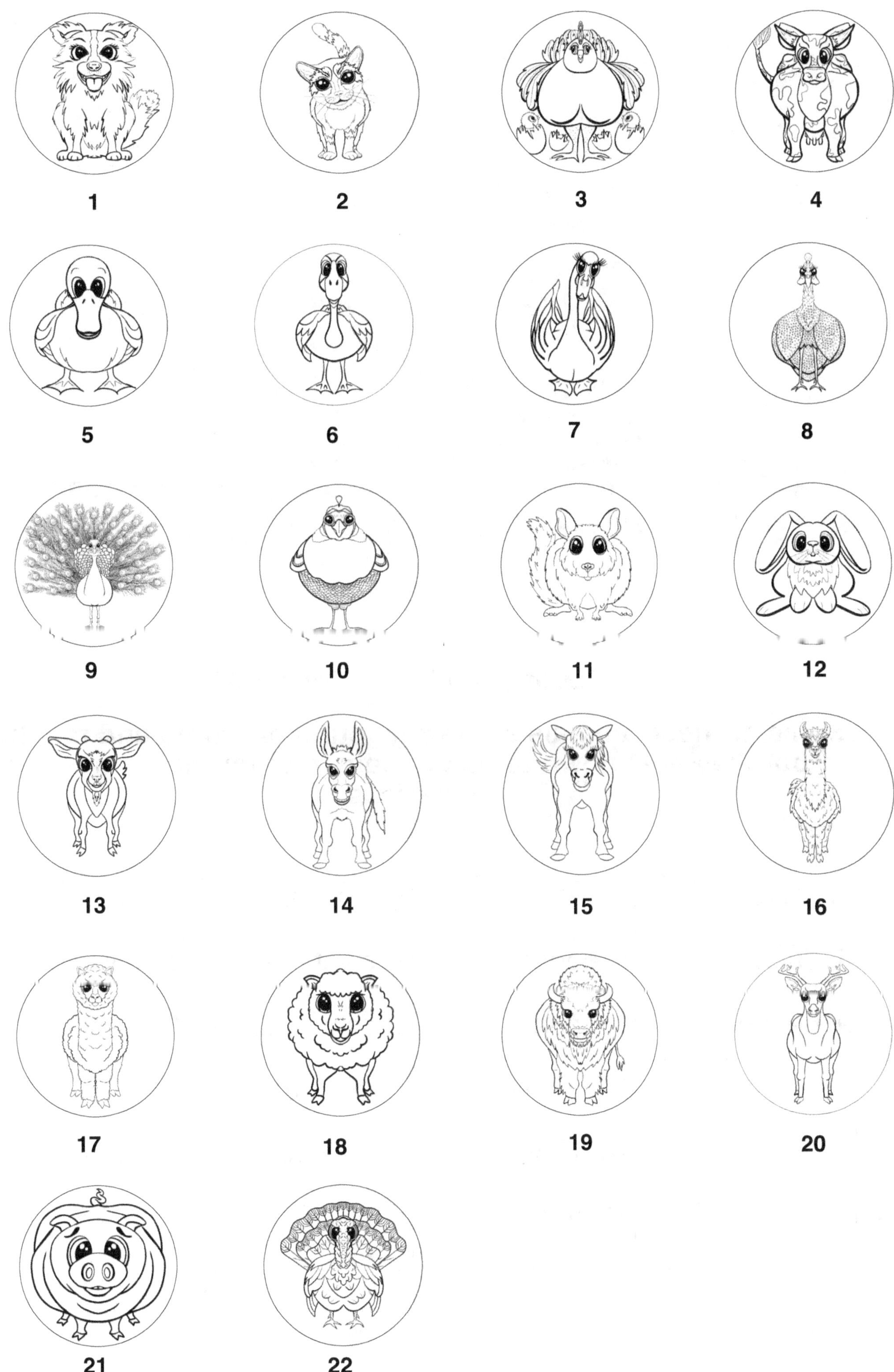

1
2
3
4
5
6
7
8
9
10
11
12
13
14
15
16
17
18
19
20
21
22

Could you identify them all?

Some of these animals are rarely found on farms and ranches, but they are known to be on them in different parts of the Americas.

1. dog	2. cat	3. chicken	4. cow
5. duck	6. goose	7. swan	8. guinea
9. peacock	10. quail	11. chinchilla	12. rabbit
13. goat	14. donkey	15. horse	16. llama
17. alpaca	18. sheep	19. bison	20. deer
21. pig	22. turkey		

The dog is an essential part of a farm and ranch.

They are not just a family pet, they protect and guard the family and they are used to guard and protect the other animals from predators that want to eat them.

They bark to alert the farmer when unwanted animals or strangers are around, and they will fight and chase away predatory animals that try to attack the animals they are guarding.

Dogs are also trained to move flocks and herds around the farm following the voice commands of the farmer.

The cat is also a welcomed animal on every farm and ranch.

They are also more than just pets. They also play a big role in protecting the farm.

Cats are helpful for keeping mice, rats, squirrels, and other rodents from damaging the farm. They protect the garden vegetables that the rodents try to eat. They protect the animals feed in the barn that rodents try to steal. Keeping the rodent population down on the farm is very helpful to the farmer and his family.

Chickens and other poultry are great assets to a farm and ranch.

Chickens provide food and protection.

Chickens are used on farms mostly to provide eggs and meat, but they can also protect the farm from damaging insects. They love to eat insects, or bugs. They are excellent at keeping roach populations low on a farm when they are allowed to roam freely. They can also keep some insects from the garden, but because they also like to eat some of the vegetables, it isn't a good idea to let them roam the garden but the outside border is helpful.

Chickens are also great composting machines. They will eat garden scraps and their manure can be used as fertilizer for the garden.

There are many people who will also tell you that chickens make great affectionate pets.

A mature female chicken is called a hen.

A mature male chicken is called a rooster.

A baby chicken is called a chick or a biddy.

Roosters are well known for their very loud crowing early in the mornings. It sounds like, "Cock-a-doodle-do!" Farmers often use them as an alarm clock, because they begin crowing when the sun rises. They can be aggressive and will sometimes chase and attack you with their sharp spurs.

Hens make a clucking sound like, "cluck, cluck, cluck." They are very protective mothers to their little chicks.

The hen will set on her nest of eggs for about 21 days to incubate and hatch her chicks.

The chicks, or biddies, make a cheeping sound like a little bird. They will sleep under their mom's soft warm feathers to stay safe and warm until they are big enough to roost with the other chickens at night.

Cattle are very often found on farms and ranches in the Americas and other countries around the world.

A herd of cattle are commonly called cows.

Cows provide milk, beef, and leather goods. Their milk can be use to make other dairy products like cheese, butter, cream-cheese, cottage cheese, buttermilk and cream.

They are herbivores that eat grass, hay, and grains. They will also eat vegetables from the garden. Some of them love watermelon too. So don't let them get too close to your garden or them will eat everything in sight.

A mature male cow is called a bull.

A young female cow is called a heifer before it becomes a mom.

A young neutered male is called a steer.

A mature female cow is called a cow.

A baby male and female cow is called a calf.

Have you ever wondered how a cow can get so fat when they only eat vegetation?

Cows make a sound like, "Moo!" when they talk.

Bulls can be very territorial and are known to attack people.

In some countries, they are used in bullfights, bull runs, and rodeos. In other countries, they are worshiped like gods.

Ducks are waterfowl. They can be found on farms and ranches and also in the wild.

Ducks are raised for their eggs and meat. Like chickens and other farm birds, ducks are great at keeping insect populations down around the farm as well as composting garden vegetation.

Like chickens, ducks eat plants, grains, and small insects.

Some people also think ducks make very affectionate pets.

A male duck is called a drake.

A female duck is called a hen.

Baby ducks are called ducklings.

Ducks make a sound like, "Quack, quack, quack!"

Ducks are great swimmers and can fly long distances.

They have also been known to eat very small fish, amphibians and reptiles.

Geese are raised on farms for meat and eggs. Their downy feathers are also used to make feather beds, comforters, and pillows.

They eat vegetation, grains, and insects. And like ducks, they are waterfowl and may occasionally eat very small fish, amphibians, and reptiles.

They can also be found in the wild. They can fly long distances.

A group of geese is called a gaggle or flock.

We call a male goose a gander.

We call a female a goose.

A baby goose is called a gosling.

Geese make a sound like, "Honk, honk!"

Although not very common, you can find swans being raised on farms and ranches.

Swans are waterfowl. They are very large and considered one of the most beautiful and graceful birds.

They are used for meat and are considered a rare delicacy in some countries where they are only eaten during a special feast.

The male swan is called a cob.

The female swan is called a pen.

A baby swan is called a cygnet.

They eat vegetation, grains, insects and sometimes very small fish, amphibians, and reptiles.

Swans make a trumpeting "Oh-oh" sound.

A group of swans is called a bevy or wedge in flight.

Swans mate for life.

Guineafowl are poultry originating from Africa and can be found on many farms and ranches in the Americas.

They are sometimes called guineas. The Helmeted guineafowl are the most popularly domesticated variety.

They are raised on farms for their eggs and meat.

They also work as an added layer of farm and ranch security against strangers and predators because they are very alert and very noisy when they sense danger.

Like other poultry birds, they eat grains, seeds, insects, and vegetation.

When they sound their alarm, it sounds like, "Pot-rack, pot-rack, pot-rack!"

Their feathers are gray and covered in tiny white polkadots.

Male guineafowl are called guinea cocks.

Female guineafowl are called guinea hens.

Baby guineafowl are called keets.

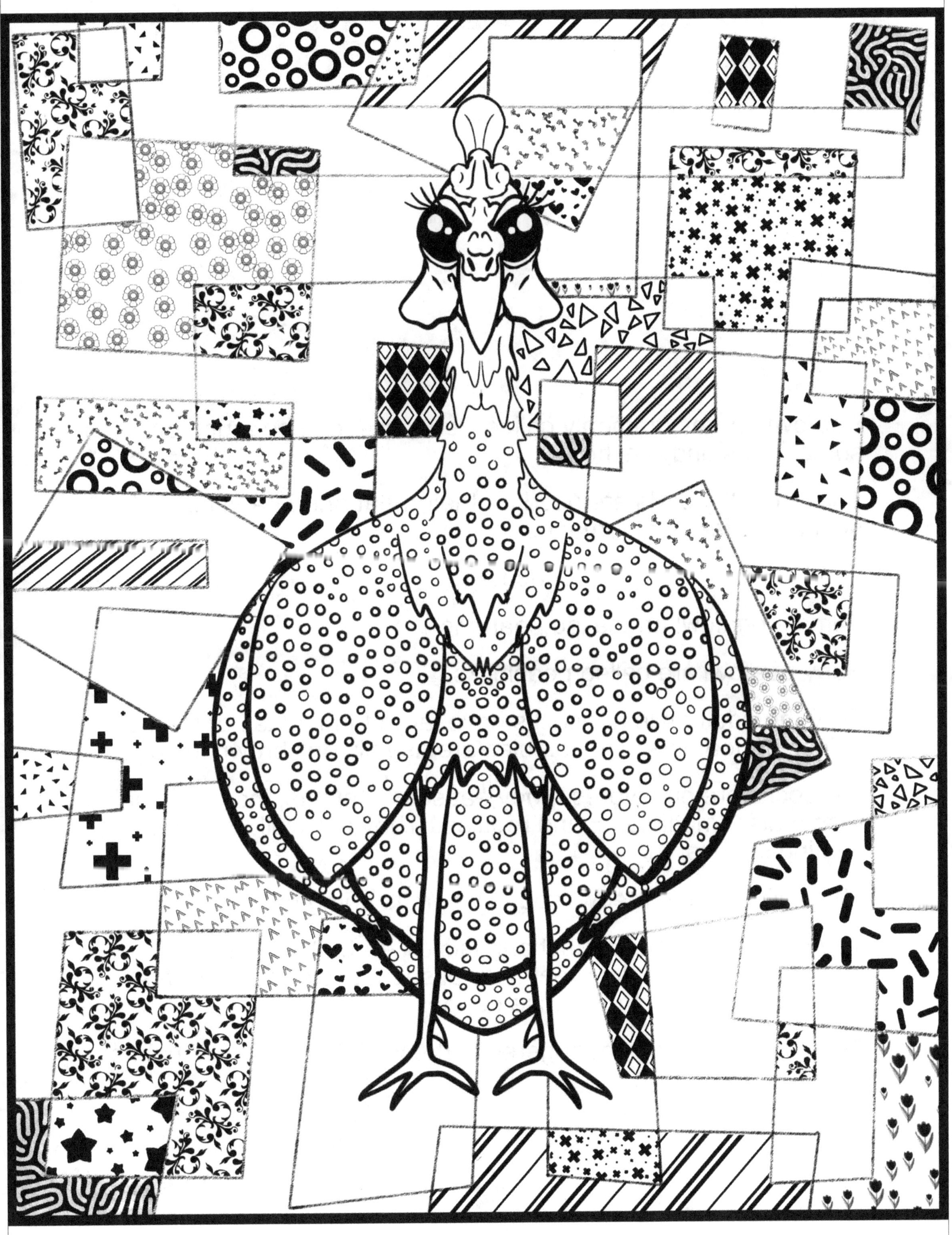

Peafowl, more commonly called Peacocks, can be found on some farms and ranches.

These poultry birds are used for their meat and beautiful, decorative feather plumage.

Male peafowl are called peacocks.

Female peafowl are called peahens.

Baby peafowl are called peachicks.

Only the adult male peacocks have large fanning tail or train of iridescent feathers. The females are usually dull brown in color.

Peacocks are omnivores. They eat seeds, plants, insects, small mammals, amphibians, and reptiles. They are well known for fighting snakes.

They will make a "meow" sound when its going to rain.

They are one of the loudest animals on earth. Like the guineafowl, they make great natural security alarms for farms and ranches when they sense danger.

They are becoming endangered in the wild due to loss of habitat.

Quail are small birds more commonly found in the wild.

They are raised on farms and ranches for their eggs and meat.

They are much smaller and more quiet than chickens and other more popular farm poultry.

A group of quails is called a covey or flock.

A male quail is called a cock.

A female quail is called a hen.

A baby quail is called a chick.

Their sound is described like a "quavering whinny" similar to the Eastern screech owl.

Pickled quail eggs are a delicious treat.

Chinchilla are rodents native to the Andes mountains in South American countries and they are currently endangered due to the fur trade.

The demand for their very soft fur has led to some people raising them on farms and ranches. But they are more commonly used as pets today due to being an endangered species.

In the wild, Chinchillas live in colonies called herds. They live in burrows and rock crevices.

They love dust baths.

Rabbits are raised on many farms and ranches.

They are mostly raised for their meat now, but were once also raised for their fur.

Rabbits are also very popular pets.

Rabbits are herbivores. They eat plants, fruits, and vegetables.

In the wild, rabbits live in burrows.

A male rabbit is called a buck.

A female rabbit is called a doe.

A baby rabbit is called a kit or kitten.

They are social animals and live in colonies.

A group of rabbits is called a herd.

Goats are very popular animals on farms and ranches.

They are raised for their meat, milk and fur.

Goats are herbivores. They eat almost everything in the plant world, but prefer woody shrubs and trees.

They are often used to clear fire hazard undergrowth in communities through grazing.

A male goat is called a billy or buck.

A female goat is called a nanny or doe.

A baby goat is called a kid.

For most breeds, both male and female goats have beards and horns.

Goats are very clever and playful animals. They love to head butt everything.

Donkeys are used on farms and ranches as guard animals as well as labor or pack animals. They can fight and kill coyotes when they threaten livestock on a farm or ranch.

They are known to be very stubborn animals. Which can make it frustrating for farmers to work with them doing farm labor duties.

Other names for a donkey is burro or ass.

A male donkey is called a Jack or Jackass.

A female donkey is called a Jenny or Jennet.

A baby donkey is called a foal.

Donkeys make a braying sound like, "Hee-haw, hee-haw!"

The offspring of a male zebra and a female donkey is called a zonkie.

The offspring of a male donkey and a female horse is called a mule.

The offspring of a male horse and a female donkey is called a hinny.

Horses are very useful animals on farms and ranches.

Horses have been used for transportation, travel, pleasure riding, therapy, rodeos, farming, racing, military cavalry, policing, packing, hauling and herding for centuries.

In some countries they are also used for meat, dog food, and soap making.

A mature male horse is called a stallion.

A mature female horse is called a mare.

A young female horse is called a filly.

A young male horse is called a colt.

A baby horse is called a foal or yearling (1-2 years old).

A neutered male horse is a gelding.

Horses make a whinny sound or a neighing sound.

A pony is a type of small horse.

Llamas are native to Peru in the Andes mountains of South America.

They are raised on farms and ranches for their work as pack animals, guards for livestock herds, and for their meat.

They like to spit when they are mad. If they are very irritated when they spit they will include a lot of stomach contents in the attack.

They are very vocal herd animals. They are known to make a sound like "Mwa," snorting, humming, clucking, screaming, screeching, and grumbling.

They make good herd guard animals.

Alpacas are cousins to the llama. They are also native to Peru. in the Andes mountains of South America.

They are also raised on farms and ranches for their wool or fur, and meat.

It is difficult for most people to distinguish them from the llama.

Alpaca have shorter more straight ears and shorter faces or snouts. Llamas have longer banana shaped ears.

Alpaca faces also have a lot more fur than lamas.

Alpacas are shorter and have more rounded bodies.

Alpacas generally hold their tails close to their bodies while the llama hold theirs up or away from their bodies.

Personalities are different too. Llamas are very confident and independent, whereas alpacas are shy and stick together as a herd when threatened by a predator. Llamas will face the predator and that is why they are often used as guards for a herd of alpacas.

Llama wool is course, while alpaca fleece is softer.and can be used in clothing, unlike the llama wool which is too rough for clothing.

A baby alpaca is called a cria.

Sheep are very common animals found on farms and ranches.

They are raised for their meat, milk and wool.

The male sheep is called a ram.

The female sheep is called a ewe.

A baby sheep is called a lamb.

Sheep and very shy and stay very close to their flock.

Sheep make the sound, "Baaa! Baaaaa!"

Sheep must be shorn or have their wool shaved off because they cannot naturally lose it and it continues to grow if left untouched.

They are herbivores who graze on grasses and plants in pastures as well as grains and hay.

Bison, or American Buffalo, have not been raised on farms and ranches for very long.

They were once entirely wild and free, but after being driven to near extinction, they were brought into ranches in an effort to preserve their species.

Buffalo are valued for their high quality lean meat. They were also once hunted for their hides and bones for creating tools, shelter, bedding, and clothing by the indigenous Native Americans.

Bison are closely related to yaks and cattle.

The beefalo is the offspring of a bison and cow.

The male bison is called a bull.

The female bison is called a cow.

The baby bison is called a calf.

Bison are still considered wild animals even on ranches. They have not been as easily domesticated as cattle. The bulls are dangerous and often unpredictable even though they appear gentle and calm.

Both male and female bison have horns.

Deer and elk are becoming more popular as livestock on farms and ranches.

Deer are raised on farms and ranches for their skin and meat.

The meat of deer is called venison.

Deer are still hunted in the wild for population control in many areas.

Deer cause many automobile accidents every year by running into the road.

A male deer is called a stag, hart, or bull.

A female deer is called a doe, hind, or cow.

A baby deer is called a fawn, kid, or calf.

A group of deer is called a herd.

The approximate age of a male deer can be estimated by the number of points or spikes on its antlers.

Female deer do not grow antlers.

Pigs, swine, or hogs, are a very popular livestock on farms and ranches.

Pigs are raised for their meat. Pork sausage, pork chops, ham, and bacon are popular meat from pigs.

Pigs are very intelligent animals. Many people think they make great pets.

Pigs make a sound like, "oink, oink, oink."

A male pig is called a boar.

A female pig is called a sow.

A baby pig is called a piglet.

Pigs make a snorting and grunting sound and when they are scared or angry they make a loud squealing sound.

Pigs are omnivores. They eat a lot of things. They eat wild plants, garden vegetables and meat.

Pig farms can be very stinky.

Turkeys are another kind of poultry that is popular on farms and ranches.

They are raised for their meat which is popular for holiday feasts. Their eggs are also eaten.

A male turkey is called a gobbler or Tom.

A female turkey is called a hen.

A baby turkey is called a chick or poult.

The long floppy red flesh that hangs over his beak is called a snood.

Male turkeys like to strut around and spread their big fan of tail feathers to impress the female turkeys.

Turkeys make a sound like, "gobble, gobble, gobble."

One of the best things about living on a farm and ranch is watching the new baby animals being born and seeing them play together.

Thanks for visiting our farm and ranch!

What is your favorite farm and ranch animal?

I hope you enjoyed visiting Farmer Mike's family farm and ranch.

I hope you learned something new about the different animals that live on farms and ranches.

And I really hope you enjoyed coloring every page of your book as much as I enjoyed creating it.

Thank you for purchasing my Farm and Ranch Animals Coloring Book!

I would love to see the results of your colored pages! If you would like to share them with me, take a photo with your phone and upload to Instagram or twitter and tag me @ArtEduTech so that I can see what a great job you did! :D

If you enjoyed this book, I invite you to check out more of my coloring books on Amazon.com. (Just type my name in the Amazon search bar.) I will be making more coloring books. Thank you again for your purchase and support.

Happy coloring!

Connect with me on Social Media:

Twitter: @ArtEduTech

Instagram: @ArtEduTech

Facebook: https://Facebook.com/ArtEduTech/

Purchase Merchandise and Apparel with my artwork at:

https://ArtEduTech.Redbubble.com/

https://candiefx.threadless.com/

www.ingramcontent.com/pod-product-compliance
Lightning Source LLC
Chambersburg PA
CBHW081559250726
48653CB00009B/3507